One Cent Magenta Creative

I'M GLAD I ASKED MY mom

A recorded conversation about life, thoughts and memories between you and your mom.

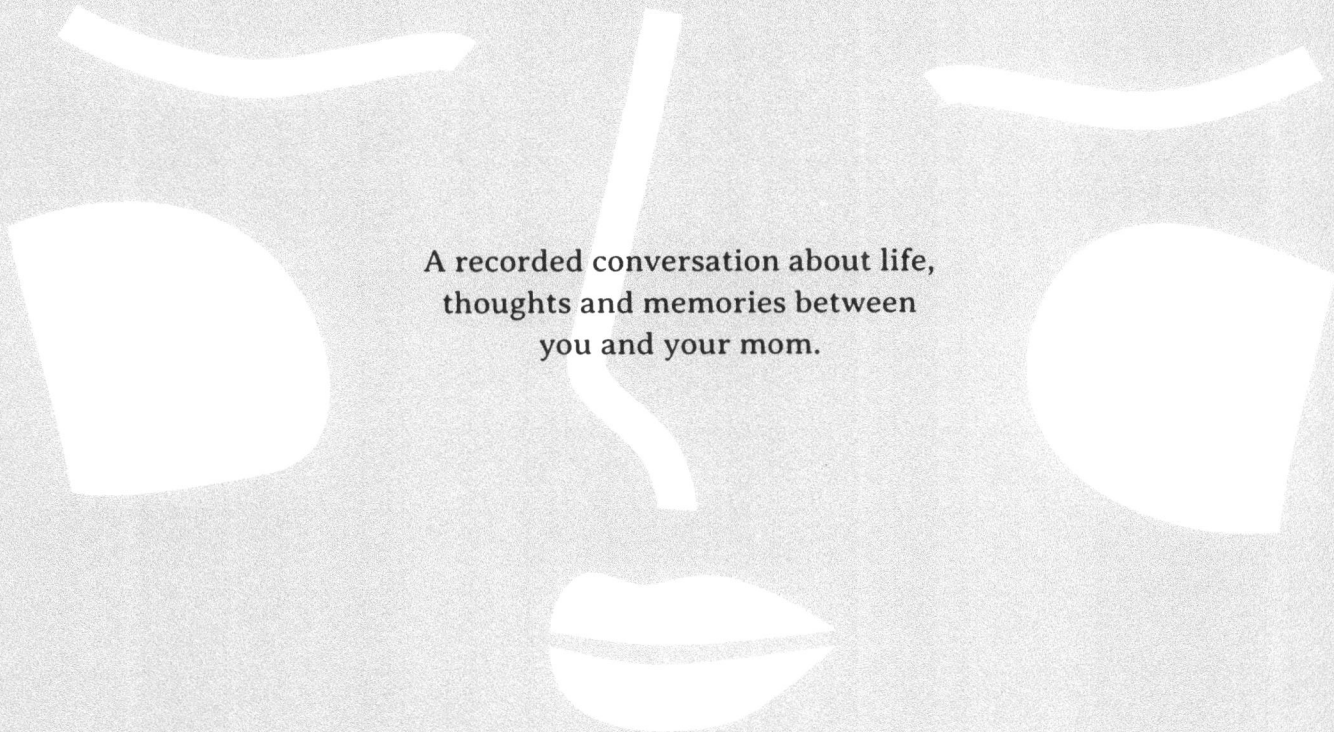

One Cent Magenta Creative

Copyright © 2020 by One Cent Magenta Creative

Published in the United States by
One Cent Magenta Creative, Chicago Illinois
and distributed in Canada, Australia by KDP and IngramSpark.

Library of Congress Cataloging has Cataloged as follows:
Title: I'm Glad I asked My Mom
Author: One Cent Magenta Creative
Description: First Edition / Chicago: OCMC 2020

Paperback ISBN 978-1-7361834-0-3

Design by Anna Pietrangeli
Illustrations by Anna Pietrangeli
Printed in the United States

For Information visit:
ImGladIAsked.com

For all those who understand it is important
to remember and appreciate their history and
treasure time spent with those they love.

ALSO BY ONE CENT MAGENTA CREATIVE

I'm Glad I Asked My Dad

I'm Glad I Asked My Grandmother

I'm Glad I Asked My Grandfather

CONTENTS

Inspired By

The creation of this series began one night when after dinner, my twenty-something son and I were sitting at the table, and started talking about life. The conversation went in many directions, but he was most interested in talking about my life, my youth, motivators, my favorite things, experiences and when looking back, what would I have changed.

The evening and the conversation touched me deeply and made me think that there were questions I never thought to ask my parents and that now they will remain unanswered. The specialness of the experience inspired me to create assemble a way that others could also have such a night and have answerers to the questions.

At the end of the conversation, we stood up and gave each other a wonderfully long hug and shed a few tears of joy and thanks.
I hope you enjoy the time spent and what is learned during your conversation.

Sincerely,

Robert Garcia

One Cent Magenta Creative

Why a written record?

A digital note or audio recording is important but difficult to hand down from generation to generation.

We hope you put your interview on a shelf and occasionally take it down, to reflect and remember.

We also hope that this passes from hand to hand and becomes a family treasure.

You are the Interviewer

This diary is designed as a guide for you as the interviewer asking the enclosed questions.

It is designed to inspire memories and for you the interviewer to gain insight into your parent's life and how they became who they are.

"Your Grandparents" - Your Moms Grandparents

"Your Parents" - Your Moms Parents

"You" - Your Mom

use blank spaces to mount photos

early years

chapter one

EARLY YEARS

WHEN & WHERE
remember the moments

Day: _____

Date: _____

Time: _____

Place and Surroundings: _____

_____

_____

Food: _____

_____

_____

Beverage: _____

_____

_____

How did the conversation happen? _____

_____

_____

_____

LET'S GET STARTED
interview time, space and menu

Your name (Subject) _____

Were you named after anyone? _____

Date of birth _____ How Old are You? _____

Where Were You Born? _____

Interviewer Name_____ Interviewer Age_____

At different ages you see things differently, so the conversation and understanding of the answer changes.

What is your favorite color?_____

What is your favorite meal?_____

What is your favorite dessert?_____

Do you have a lucky number?_____

Do you have a favorite season?_____

Did you have a nickname growing up?_____

Where did it come from?_____

Your best friends name?_____

How long have you known each other?_____

Where and how did you meet?_____

Growing up you lived at what address(s)?

Street _____

City and State _____

Phone Number (_____) _____ - _____

Street _____

City and State _____

Phone Number (_____) _____ - _____

What was it like?

_____

_____

_____

_____

Why did your parents choose this place?

_____

_____

_____

_____

Your Brothers and Sisters

Name:_____ Birthdate:_____

Name:_____ Birthdate:_____

Name:_____ Birthdate:_____

Name:_____ Birthdate:_____

Name:_____ Birthdate:_____

Name:_____ Birthdate:_____

_____

_____

_____

_____

_____

_____

_____

_____

_____

_____

_____

SCHOOL YEARS

Your middle school was? _____

_____

Your High School was? _____

_____

How did you get to school? _____

_____

What was your favorite subject (s) _____

_____

When did you graduate from High School? _____

_____

What did you wear to High School? _____

_____

Did you have any jobs when you were in High School?

   1 _____

   2 _____

   3 _____

What were you paid? _____

_____

What did you spend your money on? _____

_____

_____

Did you have any childhood idols or heros? _____

_____

_____

_____

What were some memories of High School? _____

Sports, clubs, friends, places you would hang out? _____

_____

_____

_____

_____

_____

_____

_____

_____

Did you go to college? _____

What college did you go to? _____

Why did you choose that school?

_____

_____

_____

_____

_____

_____

What did you major in? _____

What are some college memories you have?

Sports, clubs, friends, places you would hang out? _____

_____

_____

_____

_____

_____

_____

_____

_____

_____

YOUR GRANDPARENTS

your conversation persons grandparents

What were Your Grandparents names, and where were they from?

Name:_____ From:_____

Name:_____ From:_____

Name:_____ From:_____

Name:_____ From:_____

_____

What was their occupation?

_____

_____

_____

What were they like? *Their personalities, interests, history*

_____

_____

_____

_____

What was their story?

_____

_____

_____

_____

_____

_____

_____

_____

_____

_____

_____

_____

_____

_____

YOUR PARENTS

your conversation persons parents

What were Your Parents names and where were they from?

Name:_____   From:_____

Name:_____   From:_____

Name:_____   From:_____

Name:_____   From:_____

What was their occupation?

_____

_____

_____

_____

What were they like? *Their personalities, interests, history*

_____

_____

_____

_____

_____

What was their story?

_____

_____

_____

_____

_____

_____

_____

_____

_____

_____

Were they strict or lenient with you?_____

_____

What is one random thing I do not know about your parents?_____

_____

What gift did your parents give you that you remember or cherish the most? _____

_____

Did your parents talk about their parents a lot?_____

_____

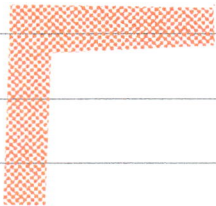
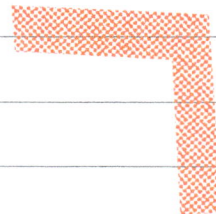

photo frame

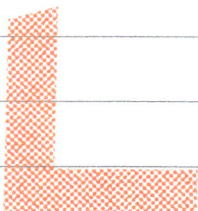

you

chapter two

YOU

What were some names of your childhood friends?

_____   _____

_____   _____

_____   _____

_____   _____

_____   _____

What TV shows did you watch growing up?

1 _____

2 _____

3 _____

4 _____

5 _____

6 _____

Did you have any pets when you were growing up?

Name_____ Type / Breed_____

Name_____ Type / Breed_____

Name_____ Type / Breed_____

Name_____ Type / Breed_____

Name_____ Type / Breed_____

What were some games you played?

Board games, outside games or around the house games_____

Game/Type_____

Game/Type_____

Game/Type_____

Game/Type_____

At what age did you go on your first airplane trip?_____

Where did you go and with who?_____

_____

_____

_____

_____

Was there a radio station(s) you listened to?_____

What city was it in?_____

What activities did you do as a kid that you liked the most?_____

_____

_____

_____

_____

What childhood activity do you miss seeing or doing the most?

_____

_____

_____

_____

_____

When you close your eyes and think of your growing up, what memories do you see?

_____

_____

_____

_____

Is there a special memory you have of My growing up?

_____

_____

_____

_____

_____

What do you remember about these key days in history?

Choose selections from Historical Moments of the Century pages 65 to 69

Event

Memory

Event

Memory

Event

Memory

SHORTS

Did you have a favorite bedtime story?

_____

_____

What historical moment stands out to you?

_____

_____

What historic event would you have liked to have witnessed?

_____

_____

What skill(s) should everyone have?

_____

_____

What is the single best piece of advice you've been given? Who Gave it to you?

_____

_____

What did you find most difficult about growing up?

_____

_____

_____

SIDE DOOR INSIGHTS

If you have an imaginary dinner party for six who would you invite? *Living or dead*

1 _____

2 _____

3 _____

4 _____

5 _____

6 _____

Have you ever been told you look like a celebrity? *If So who?* _____

What are the three things you would bring to a deserted island?

1 _____

2 _____

3 _____

If you were to have a superpower what would you want it to be?

_____

What time period and place would you have liked to have lived in?

_____

What is a pet peeve of yours that sounds silly but really gets you?

_____

What are three of your favorite movies?

1 _____

2 _____

3 _____

Did you have a favorite actress or actor?

_____

_____

_____

Do you have a favorite book(s)? Did they have an effect on you?

_____

_____

_____

What are three of your favorite songs?

Song _____

   Artist _____

Song _____

   Artist _____

Song _____

   Artist _____

Is there a song or book title that best describes you?

Song / Book

Artist / Author

photo frame

What would a perfect day look like to you?

Where, who, with and doing what

in your

20's
_____
_____
_____
_____

30's
_____
_____
_____
_____

40's
_____
_____
_____
_____

50's _____

_____

_____

_____

_____

60's _____

_____

_____

_____

_____

Now _____

_____

_____

_____

MORE SHORTS

What clothing fad did you best enjoy as a kid?

_____

What year would that have been?

What is the place you have visited that you thought was most beautiful?

_____

Is there any place in the world that you would like to visit?

Is there any place in the world where you wish you could live? Why there?

_____

_____

If you could remain one age forever what age would you choose?

_____

_____

What is one random thing I do not know about you?

_____

_____

Have you ever been in a serious accident?

_____

_____

Where did you and_____**meet?**

Mom, Dad, Grandma, Grandpa, Partner?

_____

_____

_____

_____

Where did you get married?

_____

_____

_____

_____

Did you go on a honeymoon? To where?

_____

_____

_____

_____

What were some jobs you held?

Place_____ Age_____

Place_____ Age_____

Place_____ Age_____

Place_____ Age_____

Did you know what you wanted to do when you were my age?

_____

_____

_____

_____

_____

When were/are you the happiest?

_____

_____

_____

_____

_____

If you could redo one day in your life, whether it be revising a day or reliving a day what day would it be and why?_____

_____

_____

_____

_____

Three words that describe you

_____

_____

_____

_____

_____

_____

_____

_____

today

chapter three

TODAY

What has recently made you laugh or smile?

_____

_____

_____

_____

What is something new that you have learned recently?

_____

_____

_____

_____

What has age taught you?

_____

_____

_____

_____

When did you feel you were really an adult?

_____

_____

_____

_____

_____

Today, what excites you?

_____

_____

_____

_____

_____

What today gives you a sense of awe?

_____

_____

_____

_____

_____

What causes are you passionate about?

_____

_____

_____

_____

If you could change one thing in the world today what would it be?

_____

_____

_____

_____

What the world needs now is...

_____

_____

_____

_____

_____

ME

Where did my name come from?

_____

_____

_____

What would my name have been if I was the opposite gender? _____

What did I do that tested you the most?

_____

_____

_____

_____

What do you hope I remember from my childhood?

_____

_____

_____

_____

What are some things you think are important for me to experience?

What is the most difficult thing about raising a child?

Are you the same parent to me that your parents were to you?

What are three relationship advice tips for me?

1 _____

2 _____

3 _____

What is your greatest dream for me?

_____

_____

_____

_____

_____

_____

_____

_____

_____

_____

reflection

chapter four

REFLECTION

What do you wish you had spent more time doing?

What do you wish you had spent less time doing?

What is the biggest risk you ever took?

_____

_____

_____

_____

_____

Did it turn out like you thought?

_____

_____

_____

_____

_____

Were there any defining moments in your life?

_____

_____

_____

_____

_____

Through the years have your priorities changed? *If so how?*

_____

_____

_____

_____

_____

What do you think has been your biggest accomplishment?

People, friendships, family, financial, spiritual

_____

_____

_____

_____

Looking back if you could change one thing what would it be?

_____

_____

_____

_____

Favorite Things

What is your favorite meal? _____

What is your favorite dessert? _____

What is your favorite candy? _____

What is your favorite beverage? _____

What is your favorite color? _____

What is your favorite flower? _____

What is your season? _____

What is your favorite animal? _____

What is your favorite bird? _____

What is your favorite holiday? _____

What is your favorite sport or activity? _____

What is your favorite modern convenience? _____

_____

_____

_____

_____

me to you

chapter five

ME TO YOU

NOW IT'S MY TURN

The three biggest things you have taught me

1 _____

2 _____

3 _____

What I admire about you

_____

_____

_____

_____

_____

_____

_____

What I am most grateful for

_____

_____

_____

_____

_____

Three words I would use to describe you

_____

_____

_____

_____

_____

_____

_____

family tree

chapter six

MY FAMILY TREE

my Great-Grandfather   my Great-Grandfather   my Great-Grandfather   my Great-Grandfather

my Great-Grandmother   my Great-Grandmother   my Great-Grandmother   my Great-Grandmother

my Grandmother   my Grandfather   my Grandmother   my Grandfather

my Mother   my Father

my Siblingm   y Sibling   my Sibling   my Sibling

Me

Your family's dates of birth and locations

Mom_____ Where_____

Dad_____ Where_____

Sibling_____ Where_____

Sibling_____ Where_____

Sibling_____ Where_____

Sibling_____ Where_____

Sibling_____ Where_____

Sibling_____ Where_____

Sibling_____ Where_____

_____

_____

_____

_____

_____

_____

_____

_____

1940

2000

1980

historical
moments

HISTORICAL MOMENTS
of the Century

There have been many standout moments in the last century, including going to the moon,

beginnings and ends of wars, landmark speeches, walls being built and walls coming down,

the first personal computers, email, beta became video then DVD then digital. Phones went

from the wall to cordless to being able to fit in your pocket or on your wrist. Ask if they

remember any of the moments listed in the following pages and what they remember about

them.

1920's
Color television invented (1926)
Roald Amundsen reaching the North Poll (1926)
Vaccine for tuberculosis created (1927)
First movie with sound (The Jazz Singer, 1927)
Charles Lindbergh's crosses the Atlantic (1927)

1930's
Amelia Earhart crosses the Atlantic (1932)
Programmable computer invented (1936)
Release of The Wizard of Oz – First color movie
(1939)

1940's
Penicillin treats first patient (1942)
Dialysis machine created (1943)
Atomic bomb dropped (1945)
The end of WWII (1945)
Defibrillator Created (1947)

1950's
The credit card created (1950)
First commercial jet flight (1952)
The first organ transplant (1954)
Rosa Parks refuses to give up her bus seat (1955)
First chemotherapy treatment (1956)
First satellite sent into orbit (Sputnik 1, 1957)
First racially desegregated school in the US (1957)
Pacemaker invented (1958)
Alaska becomes the 49th state (1959)
Hawaii becomes the 50th state (1959)

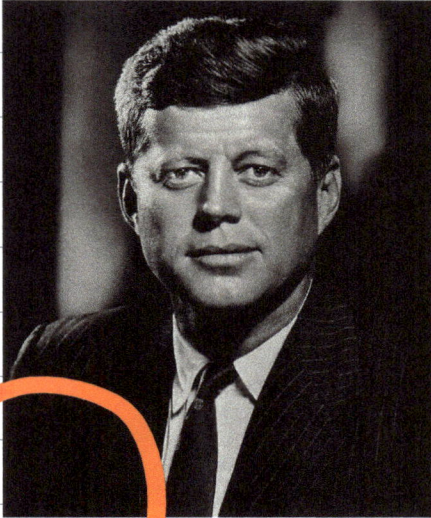

1960's

Development of the contraceptive pill (1960)
John Glen first American to orbit the earth (1961)
President Kennedy assassinated (1963)
Martin Luther King's "I Have a Dream" speech (1963)
Instant-color camera film (1963)
The civil rights acts passed (1964)
First heart transplant (1967)
Woodstock Music Festival (1968)
Martin Luther King assassinated (1968)
Bobby Kennedy assassinated (1968)
First supersonic Concorde flight (1969)
First person walks on the moon (Neil Armstrong, 1969)

1970's

Kent State students shot by guardsman (1970)
First personal computer was designed (1970)
First email sent (1971)
Walt Disney World opens (1971)
Olympic athletes taken hostage (1972)
First mobile phone conversation (1973)
Roe vs Wade decision made (1973)
Nixon resigns from office (1974)
Invention of GPS (Roger L Easton, 1974)
First female President (Isabel Peron, Argentina, 1974)
First digital camera (1975)
Saigon falls and ends Vietnam war (1975)
Apple releases its first computer (1976)
Photographs sent from Mars (1976)
First MRI scan of a human being (1977)
First "test tube baby" conceived using IVF (1978)
First person to climb Everest without oxygen (1978)

65

1980's
Invention of the Compact Disc (1980)
John Lennon is shot by Mark David Chapman (1980)
President Ronald Reagan is shot by John Hinkley (1981)
Michael Jackson debuts the moon walk (1983)
First laser eye surgery for vision correction (1983)
World Wide Web created (1983)
The Aids Epidemic (The decade)
Live Aid concert (1985)
Reagan and Gorbachev meet for first time (1985)
Space shuttle Challenger explodes on liftoff (1986)
Black Monday stock crash (1987)
Berlin Wall came down (1989)
World Wide Web created (1989)

1990's
Nelson Mandela released from prison (1990)
Persian Gulf Ware st arts (1991)
First text message sent (1992)
Branch Davidian, Waco Texas standoff (1993)
Amazon.com is born (1994)
Oklahoma City bombing of federal building (1995)
Mobile phones become popular (1995)
First cloned mammal (1996)
Google is launched (1998)
President Clinton impeachment charges (1998)

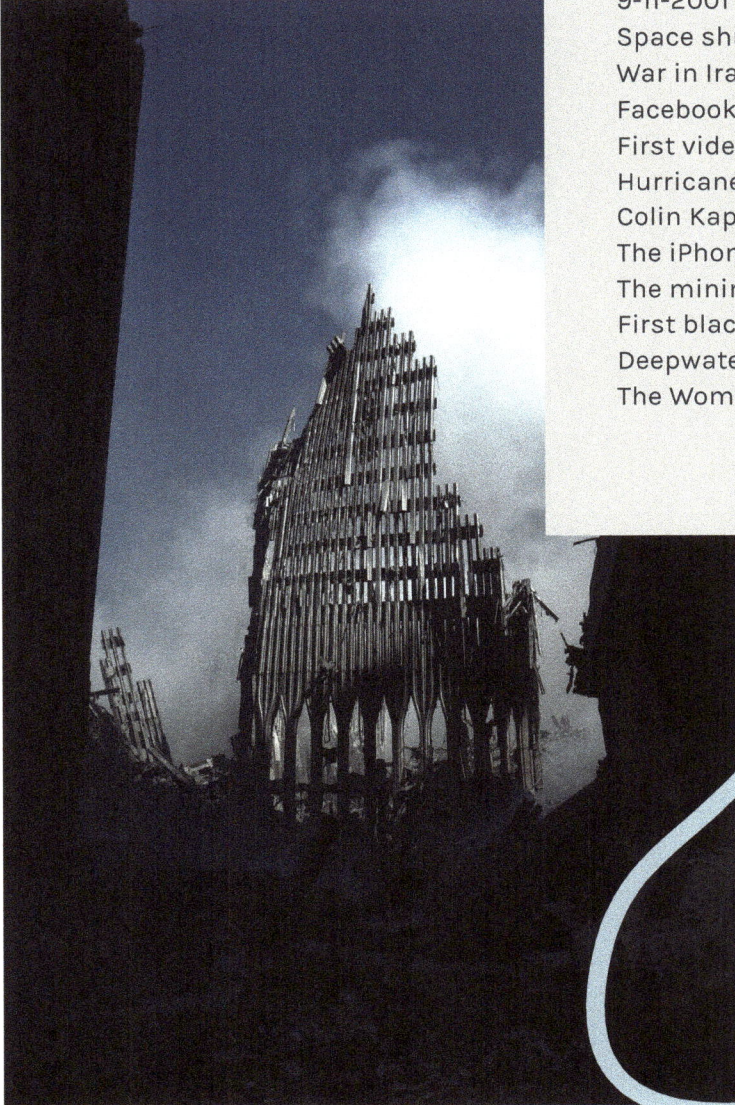

2000's
International Space Station opens (2000)
Al Gore and George Bush election has no clear winner (2000)
9-11-2001 (2001)
Space shuttle Columbia explodes during reentry (2003)
War in Iraq starts (2003)
Facebook is founded (2004)
First video to be uploaded to YouTube (2005)
Hurricane Katerina hits New Orleans (2005)
Colin Kapernick takes a knee (2016)
The iPhone is released (2007)
The minimum wage in the US increases to $5.85 / hr (2007)
First black US President elected (Barack Obama, 2008)
Deepwater Horizon oil spill in Gulf of Mexico (2010)
The Women's March (2017)

One Cent Magenta Creative

Once Cent Magenta Creative is named after the one-of-a-kind rarest and most valuable stamp in the world in which there is only one known to exist.

Like the stamp, the creative team at One Cent Magenta Creative finds rare and unique solutions in the areas of art, design, marketing, and publishing. The collective comprises designers, builders, thinkers, and artists whose goal is crafting forwarding thinking creative products.

The One Cent Magenta

The British Guiana 1 Cent Magenta is the world's most famous and rarest stamp. It was issued in British Guiana (now Guyana) in 1856, and only one specimen is now known to exist.

It is printed in black on magenta paper, and it features a sailing ship along with the colony's Latin motto "Damus Petimus Que Vicissim" (We give and expect in return) in the middle. The last four times it was sold It has broken the world record for a single stamp at auction. It last sold in June of 2014 for $9,480,000 US.

Design by Anna Pietrangeli
Illustrations by Anna Pietrangeli

www.ingramcontent.com/pod-product-compliance
Lightning Source LLC
Chambersburg PA
CBHW042354030426

42336CB00029B/3476